Science

Look How
It Changes!

By June Young

Subject Consultant
Andrew Fraknoi
Chair, Astronomy Program
Foothill College
Los Altos Hills, California

Reading Consultant
Cecilia Minden-Cupp, PhD
Former Director of the Language and Literacy Program
Harvard Graduate School of Education
Cambridge, Massachusetts

Children's Press®
A Division of Scholastic Inc.
New York   Toronto   London   Auckland   Sydney
Mexico City   New Delhi   Hong Kong
Danbury, Connecticut

Designer: Herman Adler Design
Photo Researcher: Caroline Anderson
The photo on the cover shows a tree changing with the seasons.

Library of Congress Cataloging-in-Publication Data

Young, June, 1954–
  Look how it changes / by June Young ; consultants, Andrew Fraknoi,
Cecilia Minden-Cupp.
       p. cm. — (Rookie Read-About Science)
    Includes index.
    ISBN 0-516-25901-6 (lib. bdg.)   0-516-28178-X (pbk.)
    1. Chemical reactions—Juvenile literature. 2. Matter—Properties—Juvenile
literature. I. Title. II. Series.
    QD501.Y68 2006
    541'.39—dc22   2005023923

Things are always changing.

Sometimes a change is
a physical change.

Look. Listen. Feel.

Something breaks.
Something melts.
Something freezes.
Something stretches.
Things change.
Yet they stay the same.

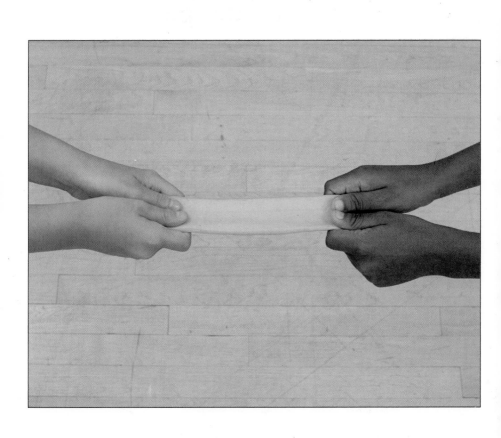

Other changes are
chemical changes.

Look. Listen.
Smell. Feel. Taste.

Something changes.
It changes into
something new.

Chemical changes happen
in autumn. Look at the
colors. Green leaves turn
red and yellow.

Watch your mom make a
fire. Leaves burn. See the
smoke. Feel the heat. The
leaves change to smoke and
ash. Things change.

Toast a marshmallow.
Hear it sizzle. See white
turn to black. Taste it on
your tongue.

The heat changes the
marshmallow to a soft,
gooey treat. Things change.

Chemical changes happen
in winter.

See the hare. In the
summer, its fur was brown.
In the winter, its fur is as
white as snow.

The hare's fur changes
to protect it from other
animals. Things change.

Pop. Crack. Sit by the fire. Smell the smoke. Feel the heat.

The fire has burned out.
See the ashes? Things change.

Chemical changes happen in spring. The sun shines. Plants take in the light. They use it to grow. Things change.

17

18

Flowers bloom. A bee
stops to eat. Sip. Sip.
What will the bee do with
the nectar from the flower?

The bee flies home to store its food. The food turns to golden honey. It feels sticky. It tastes sweet. Things change.

21

Rain falls.

Who left the bike outside? It has been outside a long time.

See the rust. Things change.

Chemical changes happen in summer. Let's boil some eggs. Let's bake a cake.

It is picnic time. Yum.
Yum. Things change.

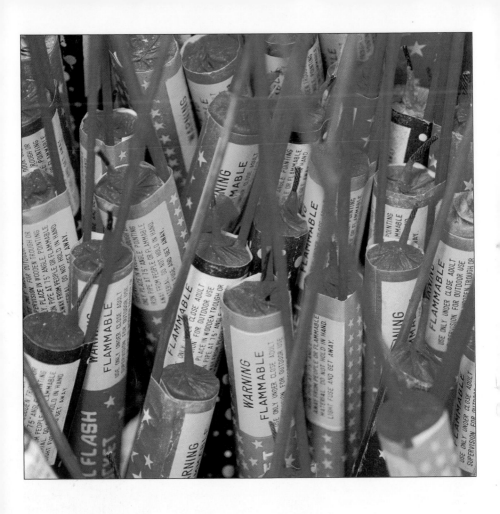

Bang. Bang. Fireworks
burst in the sky.

Hear the loud sounds.
See the bright colors.
Things change.

Look. Listen. Smell.
Feel. Taste. Things are
always changing.

Words You Know

chemical change

hare

marshmallow

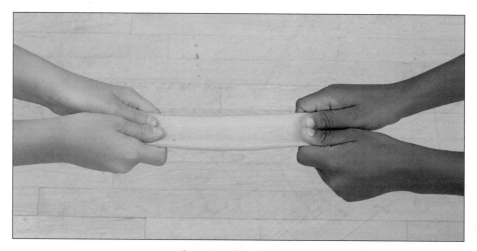

physical change

rust

Index

About the Author

June Young lives in Austin, Texas, where things change all year long.

Photo Credits

Photographs © 2006: Corbis Images: 17 (Steve Austin/Papilio), 18 (Ralph A. Clevenger), 6, 30 top (Anna Clopet), 27 (P. Freytag/zefa), 21 (Michelle Garrett), 9 (Philip Gould), 8 (Robert Llewelyn/zefa); Dembinsky Photo Assoc./Dick Scott: 13 top; Envision Stock Photography Inc./Steven Mark Needham: 24; Getty Images: cover (Rich Iwasaki/Stone), 15 (Bruce Laurance/Photodisc), 22, 31 bottom (Pat Powers & Cherryl Schafer/Photodisc), 26 (Photodisc Collection); James Levin Studios: 3, 5, 25, 29, 31 top; Photo Researchers, NY: 13 bottom, 30 bottom left (Michael Giannechini), 14 (Blair Seitz); Superstock, Inc./John A. Rizzo/age fotostock: 10, 30 bottom right.